Literary Newsmakers for Students, Volume 2

Project Editor
Anne Marie Hacht **Editorial**
Ira Mark Milne

Rights Acquisition and Management
Margaret Chamberlain-Gaston and Robyn Young
Manufacturing
Rita Wimberly

Imaging
Lezlie Light, Mike Logusz, and Kelly Quin
Product Design
Pamela A. E. Galbreath **Vendor Administration**
Civie Green **Product Manager**
Meggin Condino © 2006 Gale, a part of Cengage Learning Inc.

For more information, contact
Gale, an imprint of Cengage Learning

agency, institution, publication, service, or individual does not imply endorsement of the editors or publisher. Errors brought to the attention of the publisher and verified to the satisfaction of the publisher will be corrected in future editions.

ISBN 13: 978-1-4144-0282-6
ISBN 10: 1-4144-0282-1
ISSN: 1559-9639

This title is also available as an e-book
ISBN-13: 978-1-4144-2930-4, ISBN-10: 1-4144-2930-4
Contact your Gale, an imprint of Cengage Learning representative for ordering information.

Printed in the United States of America

10 9 8 7 6 5 4 3 2 1

My Sister's Keeper

Jodi Picoult

2004

Introduction

Jodi Picoult's *My Sister's Keeper* (2004) explores the medical, legal, ethical, and moral issues related to long-term illness—a complicated subject in the contemporary world. In the book, thirteen-year-old Anna sues her parents for the right to control her body. Conceived as a sibling donor match for her sister Kate, who suffers from leukemia, Anna has undergone numerous procedures to provide Kate with whatever she needs to fight her disease, but when Anna learns she is to give up a kidney for her sister, Anna hires a lawyer and takes her parents to court.

Picoult's idea for *My Sister's Keeper* came while doing research for her novel *Second Glance* (2003), when she was intrigued by information about eugenics in the United States in the 1930s. Supporters of eugenics wanted to improve the human race by allowing only those with desirable genetic characteristics to reproduce. Picoult also learned about stem cell research and linked the ideas, wondering if stem cell research could become human genome research. The related issues are complex and emotional.

A news story about a mother in Colorado who conceived a child so that the baby could donate cord blood to save the life of his elder sister also captured Picoult's imagination. The author took the idea to the next level and added more invasive procedures to increase the story's drama and ethical dilemma.

Picoult's personal experience also shaped the plot. Her middle child, Jake, had ten surgeries in three years beginning when he was six years old. Picoult's son suffered from cholesteatoma—a benign but potentially fatal tumor that can grow into the brain—in both ears. Because of this experience, Picoult understands the lengths to which a mother will go to protect her child and also how needs of a sick child are demanding for the entire family.

My Sister's Keeper won a 2005 Alex Award

from the Margaret Alexander Edwards Trust, and *Booklist* named it as one of the top ten adult books for teenagers. Reviewing the novel in *Booklist*, Kristine Huntley concluded, "This is a beautiful, heartbreaking, controversial, and honest book."

Author Biography

Jodi Picoult was born on May 19, 1966, in Long Island, New York, the daughter of Myron and Jane Picoult. She had a happy childhood growing up with her younger brother, Jonathan, in Nesconset, New York, on Long Island. Picoult began writing stories when she was young and continued the practice throughout her childhood. She also put her love of books to work with a job as a library page.

While a student at Princeton University, Picoult studied creative writing with such luminaries as Mary Morris and Robert Stone. During her student years, she published two short stories in *Seventeen* magazine. After earning her bachelor's degree in English in 1987, Picoult held several jobs. She worked for a brokerage firm on Wall Street as a technical writer, as a copywriter at a two-person advertising agency, and as a textbook editor. While teaching creative writing at a Massachusetts middle school, she earned her master's degree in education from Harvard in 1990. Picoult left the post in 1991 to focus on writing.

Picoult began writing what became her first novel while pregnant with her first child. *Songs of the Humpback Whale*, which focuses on the idea of love, was published in 1992. Picoult's second novel, *Harvesting the Heart* (1993), was based on her experiences as she tried to balance her children's needs with her writing. After the birth of her third child, Picoult made motherhood her focus and considered writing her hobby.

The author continued to write novels regularly as her children grew older. The focus of her work also evolved. Beginning with *Picture Perfect* (1995), she wrote about social issues—in this case, spousal abuse—and began receiving significant critical attention. Well-researched books became a hallmark of Picoult's work. For example, she spent a considerable amount of time exploring suicide pacts for the failed agreement at the center of *The Pact* (1998), the molestation of children by priests and related legal issues for *Perfect Match* (2002), and ghost hunters for *Second Glance* (2003).

Inspired by news items about designer babies, gene therapy, cloning, and old eugenics policies, Picoult wrote *My Sister's Keeper* (2004). The novel spent weeks on the *New York Times* bestseller list. She followed with *Vanishing Acts* (2005) and *The Tenth Circle* (2006). As of 2006, Picoult makes her home in Hanover, New Hampshire, with her family. Picoult focuses on her writing and makes numerous appearances across the United States each year.

Plot Summary

Prologue

My Sister's Keeper opens with a brief prologue. Unlike the rest of the book, this section does not reveal the speaker's identity, leaving readers to wonder whether the speaker is Anna or her sister, Kate. The narrator recalls that for the whole of her life, she existed only in relation to her sister, whose death was a favorite fantasy for her throughout childhood. She says she has come to see her sister's death as a suicide.

Section I: Monday

Part 1: Anna

Thirteen-year-old Anna pawns her necklace to raise money. She tells readers that she was created specifically to save her sister, Kate. Anna thinks of herself as a freak and of her life as abnormal. Neither she, nor Kate, nor their elder brother Jesse, had really been allowed to be children because of Kate's illness. When she was two years old, Kate was diagnosed with acute promyelocytic leukemia (APL). Anna is a perfect sibling match. Over the years, she has been hospitalized almost as often as Kate, as she has donated stem cells and bone marrow to her sister. Their family life has been focused on keeping Kate alive and reacting every time her symptoms come back.

She describes Jesse, who lives in an apartment over the family garage and is "a borderline delinquent, but he's brilliant." He drives Anna to the office of Campbell Alexander, a lawyer she wants to help her sue her parents for control over what happens to her body. It was for this purpose that she pawned the necklace.

Part 2: Campbell

At first, Campbell believes Anna and her suit are a waste of time. After he learns that her mother wants to make Anna donate a kidney to save Kate, he becomes more intrigued. Anna tells him what she has done for her sister over the years, that her parents are not listening to her about the current problem, and that she can accept that her sister will die without the transplant. He agrees to take her case. Campbell uses a service dog, but he is neither blind nor mobility impaired.

Part 3: Sara: 1990

In a first-person present-tense flashback, Sara tells of Kate's diagnosis with APL. Sara used to be a lawyer, but gave up her career to stay at home with her children, four-year-old Jesse and two-year-old Kate. Brian, her husband, works as a firefighter. Sara and Brian are shocked by Kate's illness and her uncertain survival. Sara tells her husband she will not allow Kate to die.

Part 4: Brian

Back in the present day, Brian describes his work as a firefighter captain and his chaotic family life: his drug-abusing son, his distracted wife, and his daughters, Kate and Anna. He notices something is wrong with Anna—she has no appetite and she is not wearing the locket that had been around her neck since he first gave it to her years earlier. Brian is an amateur astronomer and has a telescope on the roof of the firehouse. Anna visits him at work and looks at stars with him. He tells her the story of Orpheus, who tried to cheat Death to keep his wife among the living.

Section II: Tuesday

Part 1: Anna

Anna is at the hospital with Kate and Sara while Kate undergoes dialysis. While there, a family friend, Sheriff Vern Stackhouse, serves Sara with the papers for Anna's lawsuit. Anna did not expect this event today, and she sneaks away in the hospital and calls Jesse to come get her. At home, Sara and Brian talk to Anna about her suit. Sara does not want to listen to Anna when she says that she does not want to lose her kidney. Her father is willing to listen, but Anna tells them she feels invisible. Later, Kate tells Anna that she values her as a friend more than as a sister. After Anna and Kate are in bed, Sara visits their room and tells her that she will talk to the judge and resolve the situation. Anna seems to agree.

Part 2: Sara: 1990

Returning to the year Kate was diagnosed with APL, Sara describes dealing with the medical realities as Kate's disease progresses. Doctors tell her that bone marrow from a genetic match could help her. Because Jesse is not a perfect match and an unrelated donor is not a good scenario, Sara concludes they must have another child.

Section III: Wednesday

Part 1: Campbell

Anna's lawyer reveals a bit about his life. Campbell lives as a bachelor with his service dog, Judge. When he arrives at his office in the morning, he is surprised to find Anna is there, cleaning doorknobs to pay for his services. Anna's mother calls and tells him that Anna is backing off from the lawsuit. Anna assures him that the suit is still on.

At the courthouse the next day, Campbell and Anna meet Sara and Brian. Campbell is surprised to learn that Sara was a lawyer and is representing herself in the case. Campbell and Sara meet with Judge DeSalvo. Sara tries to tell the judge the case is off, but Campbell insists that Anna wants to proceed. Anna is called in to speak with the judge.

Part 2: Anna

Crying, Anna tells the judge that she cannot donate a kidney to Kate. After a brief discussion, the judge decides the suit will proceed and a guardian ad litem (GAL) will be appointed to ensure Anna's interests are being served. Because of Kate's health, Sara gets the judge to agree hold the hearing the following Monday. Campbell is concerned that Sara will unduly influence Anna, so the judge insists that Sara cannot talk about the case with Anna. Things are tense when the family gets home.

Part 3: Jesse

Emphasizing his bond with Anna, Jesse talks about his interests, primarily starting fires. A homeless man helps him store the chemicals he has been using to commit arson. He sets a fire in an abandoned storage facility and watches as the fire department puts it out. When Jesse gets home, he finds that Kate has become extremely ill and his mother needs him to drive them to the emergency room. Kate is in end-stage kidney disease.

Part 4: Sara: 1990–1991

In this flashback, Sara describes her pregnancy with Anna from an embryo selected because it was a perfect genetic match for Kate. Sara admits that during her pregnancy, she has only thought of the baby in terms of what it will do for Kate. She and Brian even go on television about their work with a geneticist to create a match for Kate, leading to hate mail. When Anna is born, Sara focuses more on her "gorgeous cord" that will help Kate than baby Anna.

Part 5: Julia

Julia has allowed her twin sister Isobel (Izzy) to move in with her after a traumatic breakup. Julia works as a GAL, and Judge DeSalvo asks her serve Anna in that capacity. Julia is not happy that Campbell is the attorney, but agrees to take the case. She takes Anna to the zoo, where they talk about the case. Anna tells her she has no life because of her sister, and while she understands that her parents want to protect Kate, no one listens to her. When Julia takes Kate home, Sara refuses to talk to Julia. Julia heads to Campbell's office with dread, where the two interact uneasily until Campbell's dog demands his attention.

Part 6: Campbell

Campbell and Julia knew each other fifteen years earlier. Focusing on Anna, Julia tells him that she is concerned about Anna living at home with Sara. Campbell shares these concerns and is ready to impose a restraining order on Sara. After he forces Julia out of his office, he describes how he knows Julia. They attended the same private high school, where they had a romance.

Campbell visits Anna's home, and the two are awkward as they get used to interacting again. He then takes the medical records for the case to Julia's apartment, where he meets Izzy. Izzy remembers him and disapproves of his presence. Campbell learns that Julia is still single. He had been the one to end their relationship, and neither seems completely over it.

Part 7: Anna

Anna gets Jesse to take her to the hospital. He formulates a plan so she can be alone with Kate. He pretends to be drunk outside of Kate's room, and his mother tends to him. Anna climbs in bed with her sister and admits to herself why she is there: "I came because without her, it's hard to remember who I am."

Section IV: Thursday

Part 1: Brian

At the firehouse, Brian thinks of his dangerous job and how he feels safer at work than at home. Julia catches Brian by surprise as he cooks breakfast for his crew, and she cannot resist helping. They talk about the case, and Brian mentions that he wants her to meet someone.

Part 2: Julia

Brian drives Julia to his house and tells her about his interest in astronomy on the way. The night before, she had gone to a neighborhood bar for the first time, trying to feel better after seeing Campbell. She stays there drinking for a long time, telling the bartender about Campbell and the rest of her sad romantic history. Julia takes Anna to the hospital hoping to talk to Kate, which Sara initially refuses to allow. When Julia does get to talk to Kate, they discuss Kate's illness, Jesse, and her relationship with Anna.

Part 3: Sara: 1996

Sara describes the time when Kate's cancer recurred after being in remission for five years. She describes her angry reaction to ten-year-old Jesse's frustrated pronouncement that "the world doesn't revolve around" Kate. She talks about the treatments for Kate, including three painful blood draws for five-year-old Anna.

Part 4: Anna

Anna sits with her parents at the hospital cafeteria while Julia talks to Kate. Sara brings up the lawsuit and tries to convince her to drop the lawsuit. Anna becomes angry because she believes her parents are not listening. In the midst of the argument, a sheriff's deputy drops off the temporary restraining order against Sara. Brian, Anna, and Sara drive to the courthouse, where a media swarm greets them. Anna tells Julia she wants to stop the suit, and the GAL goes in to talk to the judge. Sitting alone with her father, he comes up with a solution: They will live at the firehouse while Anna figures things out. The two of them leave without telling anyone.

Part 5: Campbell

Campbell meets with the judge, who is angry about the restraining order. Though Sara admits to ignoring the judge's order, Julia believes that Anna needs her mother. The judge warns Sara not talk about the case with Anna again. Campbell and Julia argue about how he is handling the case and Anna until his dog demands Campbell's attention.

Part 6: Jesse

Jesse meets Julia, who asks him about his sisters while he tries to ask her out. He tries to be glib, but instead tells her about how his Christmas was ruined when he was twelve because of Kate's illness.

Part 7: Brian

As Anna settles in at the firehouse, Brian tries to make her feel comfortable. When there is an emergency call in the middle of the night, Anna rides with her father and helps out. They later watch a meteor shower together on the roof of the firehouse.

Section V: Friday

Part 1: Campbell

Campbell visits Dr. Peter Bergen, the head of the medical ethics board at the hospital. Though Campbell has received Kate's medial records, he also wants Anna's. He learns that Anna's eight procedures were not reviewed by the ethics committee.

Elsewhere in the hospital, Campbell comes across Julia. They share a little information related to the case, including that Kate's doctor thinks she is too sick to benefit from a kidney transplant. Campbell suggests they meet for coffee to discuss it in depth, but Julia refuses. As she leaves the hospital, Campbell and his service dog follow. They go to her uncle's restaurant and talk about the case and why he took it.

In an inner monologue, Campbell recalls how he and Julia broke up soon after she met his parents. He imagines she believes the reason was that his parents disapproved, but that was not it.

During the meal, Anna calls from the police station. Campbell and Julia meet her there. Jesse has been arrested for stealing a judge's car. Campbell deals with the case and gets Jesse out of jail. Driving Anna home, Campbell asks her if the case is still in progress and emphasizes she must act more like an adult if the case is to move forward.

Part 2: Brian

At the firehouse, Brian tells Campbell that he supports Anna's position and will say as much to the judge at the hearing. Campbell tells Brian about Jesse's arrest.

Part 3: Sara: 1997

Sara talks about a time she had to take Anna to the emergency room for stitches after she fell off her bike. Soon after, Kate has another relapse and needs a bone marrow transplant. Sara has to give Anna ongoing injections to prepare for a procedure to harvest the bone marrow for Kate. After the operation, she wants to stay with Kate even though Anna asks for her. Brian gives Anna a locket, telling her, "I thought you deserved your own gift, since you were giving one to your sister." Sara and Anna shave their heads to cheer Kate, who is bald from her treatment.

Section VI: The Weekend

Part 1: Jesse

Jesse steals a dump truck and finds the homeless man with his chemical supplies. He asks the man, Duracell Dan, to come with him when he sets this fire. Jesse remembers another episode in his childhood when Kate's illness ruined plans he had looked forward to. Jesse sets fire to a shed, but Dan tells him that a homeless man named Rat lives there. Though the fire is roaring, Jesse goes in, pulls Rat out, and runs away.

Part 2: Anna

Anna is at the hospital with her mother and Kate. Kate's doctor, Dr. Chance, informs them that Kate is in renal failure and only has about a week to live. Later, at the firehouse, Anna talks to Julia about boys and her relationship with her sister. Sara calls to wish Anna goodnight. Anna cannot sleep that night and reads on the firehouse roof until her father joins her and they talk about the stars.

Part 3: Brian

On Sunday morning, Brian visits Kate and Sara in the hospital. He remembers what his marriage to Sara used to be like. He tells Sara that he supports Anna's point of view in the case, a point they both know could change everything.

Part 4: Sara: 2001

Sara remembers when Kate was suffering from graft-versus-host disease, which suddenly led to hemorrhaging throughout her body. The only treatment left is giving her arsenic. Sara is upset to learn that Brian wants to take Kate home to die. Kate endures, though she develops an infection and her doctor believes she will die soon. Sara feels Kate fighting back. Meanwhile, Anna reveals that she has been playing on an ice hockey team and Jesse gets in trouble for blowing up the school's septic tank. Sara discovers that Jesse has been getting blood drawn regularly to help Kate.

Part 5: Anna

Campbell, Anna, Brian, and Sara meet in Campbell's office. Sara offers a deal: If Anna gives Kate her kidney, Anna will never have to give anything else to Kate. Anna refuses.

Part 6: Julia

Campbell goes to Julia's apartment to talk about the situation. He takes Julia to dinner on a sailboat and tells her what happened with Anna and her parents. Julia feels he is trying to manipulate her to get Anna to accept her mother's bargain as the best solution. The two make love despite her suspicions, yet it feels natural and easy.

Section VIII: Monday

Part 1: Campbell

In the morning, Campbell leaves Julia sleeping on the boat with the keys to his car. He arrives at court early, as does Sara, but Anna is not there. Campbell finds her with Kate at the hospital, and he drives her to court. He demands to know why they are taking on the suit at all, and she responds by demanding to know about his service dog. He tells her that his hearing was damaged by medication for an ear infection, and he needs the dog to keep him safe. He keeps the dog's purpose a secret because he does not like people feeling sorry for him. Anna admits, "I came to your office because just for once, I wanted it to be about me instead of Kate."

When they arrive at court an hour and a half late, Campbell lays out his case, beginning by stating that it is both a legal and moral case. He questions Sara about the circumstances of Anna's conception and asks her if Anna gave her consent for any of the many often painful procedures she went through to help Kate. He points out that she has favored one child, Kate, over another, Anna, each time.

Part 2: Anna

During a court recess, Anna tells Campbell that she knows that a court victory does not really mean that she wins. She then watches Campbell as he questions Dr. Bergen. When Campbell asks why the ethics committee has never met on her case, Bergen points out that Anna has not been treated as a patient though she has undergone a number of procedures. Campbell questions the hospital's ethics regarding Anna. Bergen admits he believes that Anna should not give up her kidney because Kate is too weak for the operation. In Sara's cross-examination, she gets Bergen to admit the transplant would not hurt Anna or put her in danger.

Part 3: Sara: 2002

Sara remembers another time when Kate was still in remission, but receiving outpatient treatment in the hospital. Kate becomes involved with another cancer patient, a boy named Taylor. Kate soon relapses and undergoes chemo and a stem cell transplant. Taylor dies the night after he takes Kate to a prom at the hospital.

Part 4: Jesse

Jesse visits Kate in the hospital. She is surprised by his visit and tells him that she will miss him. Jesse asks Kate if she is afraid to die.

Part 5: Brian

Investigating yet another arson, Brian comes across a cigarette butt that leads him to suspect Jesse. He finds chemicals at Jesse's apartment, and he confronts him about them, as well as the cigarette butt, which he calls Jesse's "calling card." Jesse does not deny that he has set the fires, and he offers a simple explanation: "I couldn't save her." Realizing that his son wants to be punished for not rescuing Kate, Brian hugs him, decides not to tell anyone, and resolves that Jesse will not set any more fires.

Part 6: Campbell

Back in court, Campbell questions Dr. Chance. Campbell says that Anna's life has been endangered for thirteen years to make sure Kate survives. The procedures, anesthesia, and drugs were potentially harmful. The kidney transplant could also harm, if not kill, her. During a lunch break, Anna leaves Julia and Campbell alone so they can talk. Julia asks him if the night they spent together meant anything, but he does not answer. When court adjourns for the day, Campbell drives Anna back to the firehouse.

Section VIII: Tuesday

Part 1: Campbell

The next day in court, Brian changes his mind on the stand and publicly supports his wife's position. When Campbell presses him, Brian admits he does not know what the right thing is to do. During a recess, Campbell tells Anna that she has to testify, though he promised her earlier that she would not have to. Anna refuses.

Part 2: Sara: Present Day

Sara cross-examines Brian, but is not sure what to say as she ponders their relationship. They reconnect during a recess, and Brian and Anna move back home that night. Brian and Sara make love.

Section IX: Wednesday

Part 1: Julia

Julia is anxious and disappointed about her night with Campbell, but she is surprised to realize that she is not angry with him. At the courthouse, she sees Campbell and Anna arguing about her refusal to testify. This leads to an argument between Julia and Campbell about the case and her opinion of him.

Part 2: Campbell

In court, Sara asks if her witness, psychiatrist Dr. Neaux, can be put on the stand first because of a time conflict. Campbell agrees. The psychiatrist has had each of the family's three children as patients and believes the parents should make the decision. Under cross-examination, Campbell gets the doctor to admit that Sara cannot make decisions in Anna's best interest because Sara will always act to protect Kate.

Part 3: Julia

On the stand, Julia testifies that no one in the family, neither Anna nor her parents, can make an unprejudiced decision about what is in the best interest of Anna's health. The judge asks for Julia's opinion about what is best for Anna.

Part 4: Campbell

As the dog whines around him, Campbell starts to see that he could win. Julia tells the judge that she cannot make a recommendation on the case. Anna tells him that she will testify.

Part 5: Anna

While noting that the dog is getting more and more agitated, Anna admits on the stand that Kate wanted her to file the lawsuit. Campbell collapses in the courtroom.

Part 6: Brian

Brian takes care of Campbell, who has suffered a grand mal epileptic seizure. Campbell tells him he has had epilepsy since he was eighteen years old and suffered head trauma in a car crash.

Part 7: Campbell

Campbell tells Julia that his dog is a seizure dog, and his seizures were the reason he abruptly ended their relationship when they were teenagers. He did not want to make her live with his illness and hold her back. She responds, "this time, you don't get to leave *me*, I'm going to leave *you*.... In another fifty or sixty years."

Part 8: Anna

Campbell convinces Anna to continue with her testimony. Anna explains that Kate wanted to die and had tried to commit suicide already. Sara cannot believe it, but Anna tells her that Kate was afraid to tell her mother that she does not want to live anymore. Kate does not want Anna to give her a kidney. Anna says that Kate wants to die, and she admits that it is what she wants, too.

Part 9: Sara

The judge decides that he needs to talk to Kate and moves the court to the hospital. After a few minutes with Kate, he tells them that he will make his decision the next day.

Section X: Thursday

Part 1: Campbell

Julia has spent the night with Campbell in his apartment. He is uncertain about what the day's events will bring.

Part 2: Jesse

Walking in the rain, Jesse decides to make a new plan to feel alive.

Part 3: Anna

Anna notes that it is raining.

Part 4: Brian

Brian remembers that it was raining the day Anna was born, and he named her Andromeda after the constellation.

Part 5: Sara

During Sara's closing statements, she tells Anna that she loves her, but she believes it is right to make Anna give Kate a kidney.

Part 6: Campbell

In his closing statements, Campbell argues that only Anna's voice should be heard. The judge decides that Anna is medically emancipated, with Campbell holding her medical power of attorney until she turns eighteen.

Part 7: Anna

After filling out paperwork, Campbell drives Anna home and they discuss who she is and who she will be when she grows up. Anna admits, "Ten years from now, I'd like to be Kate's sister."

Part 8: Brian

At the hospital, Brian is called to the scene of a car accident. There, he finds Anna has suffered a severe closed head injury when a pickup truck crashed into Campbell's car. Brian rescues Campbell, Judge, and Anna from the car. Anna is brain dead, and Campbell instructs the staff to harvest a kidney for Kate.

Part 9: Sara

Sara and Brian visit Anna and accept the truth. They turn off their daughter's respirator and stay with her until she dies.

Epilogue: Part 1: Kate: 2010

Kate says that she once believed that Anna's death was her fault. Kate hated herself, Sara looked for signs that Anna was still present, and Brian consoled himself with drinking. The transplant almost failed, but Kate got better and her cancer has been in remission for eight years. Though it was hard, the family eventually let go of their grief. Jesse became a policeman, Campbell and Julia got married, and Kate works as a dance teacher. Kate feels that Anna is a part of her, and she works to preserve every memory of her.

Media Adaptations

- *My Sister's Keeper* was released as an unabridged audiobook by Recorded Books in 2004. Its readers include Julia Gibson, Barbara McCullough, and Richard Poe.

Characters

Campbell Alexander

Campbell Alexander is the lawyer Anna hires to represent her in her lawsuit. Though Campbell is initially reluctant to take the case, he ultimately decides to do so. He believes the case will be easy to win and will bring him publicity. Throughout *My Sister's Keeper*, Campbell seems to act primarily in his own self interest. He also keeps people at a distance, focusing on his career and living the bachelor life with his service dog, Judge.

Both Julia and Anna push his boundaries. Campbell was involved with Julia fifteen years earlier when they were seniors at an exclusive private high school, The Wheeler School, and have not seen each other since. Raised by rich, self-absorbed parents, the young Campbell was attracted to Julia, an outsider. After being intimately involved with Julia, he let the relationship end without telling her why. In the novel, it is revealed that he was in a car accident after a date with her and shortly before graduation. The accident left him with epilepsy, a condition he has hidden from everyone. Judge warns him when he is going to have a seizure. Campbell let Julia go so his illness would not hold her independent spirit back.

Julia and Campbell work together on Anna's case when Julia is appointed to be Anna's guardian ad litem (GAL). Campbell ultimately wins Anna's case and becomes the holder of her medical power attorney until she is eighteen years old. However, leaving the courthouse after the decision has been reached, Campbell's car is hit by a truck. Anna dies, and Campbell and Judge are hurt. He decides that Kate should receive her sister's kidney after all, a decision that saves Kate's life. Campbell and Julia eventually marry.

Taylor Ambrose

Taylor Ambrose is the sixteen-year-old cancer patient whom Kate became involved with when she was fourteen years old. They met while he was receiving chemotherapy and she was getting platelets to boost her immune system. Because of the relationship, Kate did not want to receive chemotherapy when her cancer returned. After Taylor and Kate attend the Providence Hospital Prom for patients, he died.

Peter Bergen

Dr. Bergen is the head of the medical ethics committee at Providence Hospital, where Kate has received all of her treatment. The doctor is a witness in Anna's court case. He reveals that he personally advised against Anna donating a kidney to Kate, but he supports the family's attempt to save Kate through this procedure.

Eldie Briggs

Eldie Briggs is the elderly woman Brian saves on a late-night ambulance call. Anna is along for the ride, and she holds the woman's hand on the way to the hospital.

Caesar

Caesar is one of the men who works under Brian at the fire station.

Nadya Carter

Mentioned in one of Sara's chapters, Nadya Carter is the television newsmagazine reporter who interviews Brian and Sara about their decision to have Anna.

Harrison Chance

Dr. Chance is Kate's primary oncologist throughout her illness. He is close to Kate and the family. He also testifies at the hearing.

Suzanne Crofton

Suzanne, also called Zanne, is Sara's older sister. She helped raise her younger sister after the death of their father. Suzanne pushed Sara to become a lawyer, while becoming a powerful businesswoman herself. While Suzanne did not support Sara's life choices and the sisters eventually drifted apart, Suzanne helps when Kate becomes ill. Suzanne also takes her sister out on occasion to get a break from the stress of her life.

DeSalvo

Judge DeSalvo is the presiding judge in Anna's case. He eventually rules in favor of Anna becoming medically emancipated from her parents.

Kerri Donatelli

Kerri works as Campbell's secretary.

Duracell Dan

Duracell Dan is the homeless man Jesse feeds in exchange for guarding the chemicals Jesse uses to set fires.

Farquad

Dr. Farquad is a specialist who treats Kate.

Anna Fitzgerald

Anna Fitzgerald is the primary character in *My Sister's Keeper*. She is thirteen years old, the younger sister of Kate and Jesse, and the daughter of Brian and Sara. Beginning with her birth, after which her cord blood was given to Kate, Anna has undergone numerous procedures to keep Kate alive. Some of these procedures have been quite painful for the young girl.

Because Kate is in renal failure and near death, Sara has decided that Anna will give her sister one of her kidneys, though Kate's doctors are not certain it will save Kate's life. Anna hires Campbell Alexander to be her lawyer and work to ensure that she has a choice about the procedure. Throughout *My Sister's Keeper*, Anna fights for this choice, though it divides her family.

Anna's family situation is difficult, at best. She shares a room with Kate, and they often have a normal sisterly relationship. Anna can be resentful of her mother and her sister, feeling that she is merely a vessel to help keep her sister alive. While Anna loves her rebellious brother and is close to her father, she feels overlooked by all of them.

Despite these difficulties, Anna does want to help her sister. When she testifies near the end of the novel, Anna reveals that she filed this suit primarily to help Kate. Kate does not want Anna's kidney and actually wants to end her fight to live. Leaving the courthouse after the victory, Anna dies in a car accident and ultimately gives the kidney that saves her sister.

Andromeda Fitzgerald

See Anna Fitzgerald.

Brian Fitzgerald

Brian Fitzgerald is the husband of Sara and

father of Jesse, Kate, and Anna. He is a fire captain. He admits that he took the job to save lives, something he does extremely well. Brian is an amateur astronomer in his free time and has a telescope on the roof of his firehouse. Brian is dedicated to his work and to his family. He generally has supported his wife in her never-ending struggle to keep Kate alive.

Brian also sees the price of Kate's illness and Sara's handling of the situation on the family. When Kate nearly dies, he is ready to let her go when Sara cannot. Such stances add to the growing divide between husband and wife. Brian also sees how Anna has suffered because of Sara's focus on Kate and the cancer. When Sara becomes upset about the lawsuit, Brian decides he will stay with Anna at the firehouse for a few days to give his daughter the space she needs.

Jesse Fitzgerald

Jesse Fitzgerald is the eldest child of Brian and Sara Fitzgerald, the brother of Kate and Anna. Jesse is a rebellious drug user with a juvenile record. His parents have given up on him. While he loves his sisters, he resents the effect Kate's illness has had on his family. Throughout the novel, Jesse remembers several times where Kate's illness has led to forgotten plans and overlooked gestures. Yet Jesse has also given blood to help Kate, driven her to the emergency room, and made her laugh when she was in pain. He also drives Anna around to help her with her lawsuit. Jesse expresses his own dissatisfaction by acting out, primarily by setting big fires with chemicals he stores with Duracell Dan. After Anna's death and Kate's recovery, he becomes a policeman.

Kate Fitzgerald

Kate is the sixteen-year-old daughter of Brian and Sara, the younger sister of Jesse and older sister of Anna. Kate has suffered from acute promyelocytic leukemia (APL) since the age of two. She was not expected to live as long as she has, but she survived primarily because of the many donations of the stem cells, platelets, and bone marrow from Anna. While her cancer has gone into remission several times, Kate has also suffered from related illness such as bone-and-graft disease and, during the main action of the novel, renal failure. Though Anna becomes medically emancipated, Kate ends up getting her kidney after Anna dies in a car accident. Kate lives, her cancer goes into long-term remission, and she becomes a dance teacher.

Sara Crofton Fitzgerald

Sara is the wife of Brian and mother of Jesse, Kate, and Anna. Sara once worked as a lawyer but she gave up her career to raise her children. Her whole life changed when Kate was diagnosed with APL. Sara became obsessed with keeping Kate alive, going so far as to create Anna, a genetic perfect sibling match whose umbilical cord blood could be used to help Kate.

Sara cannot understand why Anna would not want to give up a kidney to save her sister. She is bewildered and angered by Anna's lawsuit. Sara cannot, or will not, see the case from Anna's perspective. Sara tries to get Anna to drop the suit, seeing it only as a ploy for attention.

Judge

Judge is Campbell's service dog. A German Shepherd, Judge is trained to detect when Campbell is about to have a seizure and warn his owner.

Luigi

Luigi is the uncle of Julia and Izzy and the owner of the restaurant where Julia and Campbell discuss Anna's case one evening.

Beata Neaux

Dr. Neaux is a child psychiatrist who has treated all of the Fitzgerald children over the years. She testifies on Sara's behalf during the hearing.

Newbell

Judge Newbell is the owner of the Humvee that Jesse steals.

Paulie

Paulie is a fireman who works with Brian at

the firehouse.

Rat

Rat is the homeless man whom Jesse saves from the burning building. The fire was set by Jesse.

Red

Red is a firefighter who works with Brian at the firehouse.

Isobel Romano

Isobel Romano, also known as Izzy, is Julia's twin sister. A jewelry designer and a lesbian, she has just moved into her sister's home after the breakup of her long-term relationship. Izzy is critical of Campbell and protective of Julia.

Julia Romano

Julia is Campbell's high school girlfriend, Anna's guardian ad litem (GAL), and Izzy's twin sister. A graduate of Harvard Law School, Julia works as a GAL, someone who ensures that children's interests are represented in court cases. Julia is reluctant to take Anna's case at first, primarily because it involves working with Campbell. She and Campbell, who called her Jewel, had an intense relationship in high school that he ended without an explanation. After the breakup, she has had only bad relationships and is not involved with anyone when she meets Campbell again.

As they work on Anna's case, the couple gets back together. As Anna's GAL, Julia challenges Campbell to see Anna as more than just a case. On the stand, Julia is unable to give a recommendation on the case because she cannot see a right choice. During the course of hearing, Campbell's seizure leads to Julia's discovery of the reason he left her years earlier. Julia and Campbell later marry.

Seven the Bartender

Seven is the bartender at the gay bar, Shakespeare's Cat, which Julia frequents. He offers a sympathetic ear as she talks about her relationships with men.

Vern Stackhouse

Vern is a sheriff's deputy. He knows the Fitzgerald family and reluctantly serves papers related to the case to Sara. Vern also works in the courthouse and knows Campbell.

Steph

Steph is a nurse that has grown close to the Fitzgeralds over the years.

Wayne

Dr. Wayne is Kate's pediatrician. He is the one who discovers Kate's low white cell count, which leads to the cancer diagnosis.

Zanne

See Suzanne Crofton.

Ethical Dilemmas

At the heart of *My Sister's Keeper* is an ethical dilemma: Should thirteen-year-old Anna be forced to give her kidney to her dying sister? Through much of the novel, it seems like Anna does not want to give Kate her kidney because she is tired of being a store of spare parts for Kate. Since she was born, Anna has undergone a number of painful procedures to save Kate's life. Kate suffers from cancer and conditions related to the illness and its treatment. Her family's life has been focused on Kate's illness and its potential recurrence during times of remission, since before Anna was born.

Indeed, Anna was created to be a perfect sibling match for Kate. The Fitzgeralds went to a geneticist who created several embryos with the couple's sperm and eggs, then figured out which one matched Kate. That embryo was implanted in Sara and became Anna. At the time, there was public controversy over their decision because Anna was seen as a "designer baby." The ethical debate led to a talk show appearance for the couple, as well as hate mail.

More than anyone else in the family, Sara sees no ethical dilemmas, neither in how Anna was created nor in making Anna suffer to try to keep Kate alive. Sara only responds to the latest crisis and the best solution at hand. When necessary, taking from Anna to give to Kate is no dilemma for her. The result is that Kate has lived longer than her doctor ever expected, but at the cost of a balanced family. The needs of Kate and her illness are put above all else, with Sara diligently guarding those interests at the expense of her husband and other children. Even Julia, the court-appointed guardian of Anna's interests, cannot make a decision on what should be done.

Anna's lawsuit brings all these issues and the ethical dilemma to the forefront. With Campbell acting as her lawyer, she seeks the right to decide whether she gives up a kidney. Anna's true motivation in her quest for medical emancipation is yet another ethical dilemma. As she reveals on the stand during the hearing, the reason that Anna has brought the lawsuit was for Kate's benefit. Kate cannot tell her mother that she does not want to have the transplant. Kate is aware of the toll her illness has had on everyone and she seems tired of fighting. In fact, she has tried to kill herself before. This situation brings up the ethical dilemma: Should Kate be allowed to die when a measure can be taken to save her life?

None of these ethical dilemmas is allowed to reach its full conclusion in the story. The novel ends with Anna suffering an injury that leads to brain death. As executor of her medical rights, Campbell authorizes the kidney transplant. Kate's cancer goes into remission, and she has a normal life. But she knows that she is alive because Anna died. She believes that one sister had to die for the other to survive, another ethical conundrum.

Control

One issue that shapes many of the characters and situations in the novel is that of control. Nearly every major character in *My Sister's Keeper* is looking for control over some part of their existence in the face of disease. Anna, for example, seems to want to control her body and what is taken from it as evinced by her lawsuit. While it is later revealed that she actually filed the suit at Kate's behest, Anna is still looking to control the situation to give her sister what she wants. Anna knows she cannot control her mother, her family, or her sister's illness, but she seeks control of her own destiny.

Kate and Sara would like control of the opposite sides of the same coin. Kate wants to control her existence and the toll she puts on her family. She would like to become a ballerina if she grows up because she believes they have control over their bodies. Sara has spent her life since the diagnosis of Kate's cancer trying to control the disease as well as Kate's life. Sara has done everything in her power, including creating Anna, in an attempt to control Kate's destiny. Sara has controlled all she could to keep Kate alive, without truly examining the consequences to herself and her family.

One of the costs of Sara's focused assault on Kate's disease is the loss of closeness with Jesse.

Both Brian and Sara have given up on Jesse, who repeatedly acts out. He loves his sisters and has done what he can to keep Kate alive, most notably giving his blood regularly to boost her platelets. But he has also moved into an apartment over the family garage to be separate from, yet still part of, his family. He sets fires to get attention and to feel a sense of control over something. Jesse knows the fires, car theft, and substance abuse are all masks for his pain, but he needs a parent to care about him. Brian reclaims control over his son when he finds evidence that Jesse set fires.

Anna's lawyer, Campbell, is also obsessed with control. He has suffered from epileptic seizures since the age of eighteen, but he keeps his condition a secret. Whenever someone asks why he has a service dog, he gives an obviously untrue answer. He allowed his condition to end his high school romance with Julia without telling her why. He controlled the situation because he believed she should be free of the burden of caring for someone with his condition.

Familial Bonds

The importance of familial, especially sibling, relationships is another underlying theme of *My Sister's Keeper*. Despite all the problems created by Kate's illness and Sara's quest to keep Kate alive, the Fitzgeralds remain a family. Though Brian and Sara have their problems, they work together to keep the family together amidst the disruptive force of Kate's illness. Even Jesse, the delinquent son, still lives at home and is there to help out when Kate is ill or Anna needs his support.

In turn, Anna helps her brother get out of jail when he is arrested for stealing the judge's vehicle. Anna also does all she can to help her sister. While the pair squabble as sisters do when they share a room, Anna files the lawsuit to give Kate what she wants. All the siblings resent what has happened to them, but respond to the needs of the others in their family when the situation calls for it. After Anna's unexpected death, the family grieves separately but eventually grows closer again.

Like Kate and Anna, Julia and her twin sister, Izzy, are close. Julia allows her to move in after a painful breakup. Izzy wants to protect her from Campbell. While Campbell's relationship with his parents is not close at all, it serves as an illuminating contrast to the Fitzgeralds and the Romanos.

Topics for Further Study

- Analyze one of the poems that open each section of the novel. How does the poem reflect the content of that section? Research the background of the poem and its poet to add depth to your arguments for a paper. For a group activity, have each person analyze one poem and one section. Share your findings and discuss the implications of the poem for the chapter.

- Research some of the ethical questions raised by the novel, focusing on a particular issue, such as creating a child specifically for its cord blood to benefit a sibling or the implications of a teenager donating an organ to a sibling or parent. Write a paper in which you take a position on the issue you choose or, for a group activity, stage a debate with students taking opposite sides of each issue.

- Research the eugenics movement of the early twentieth century, one topic that Picoult said inspired her to write *My Sister's Keeper*. Write a paper in which you compare and contrast the goals of the eugenics movement with the choices made in the novel.

- In the novel, Picoult describes the action from multiple points of view, focusing on Anna, Sara, Brian, Campbell, and Julia. Jesse's voice appears much less often in the text than these voices, and Kate's voice only appears in the prologue and epilogue. Write a short story in which you more fully elaborate Jesse's point of view on the action or take Kate's perspective on what happens.

- Some critics were disappointed in the ending of *My Sister's Keeper*. Were you let down that the complex ethical issues presented were not resolved? If not, write a brief essay explaining why you found the ending satisfying. If so, outline a different ending and epilogue in which Anna lives. Discuss different opinions in a group.

Multiple Points of View

One striking feature of *My Sister's Keeper* is the way Picoult uses multiple first-person narrators to tell the story. A first-person point of view tells the story from one character's perspective in his or her own voice. Each section in the novel is made up of parts designated by the name of the character whose voice and perspective is being revealed. Picoult emphasizes the differences in these voices through the use of different fonts for different characters.

The use of multiple voices allows readers the ability to understand the situations from different standpoints. The way Sara sees Kate's cancer and Anna's lawsuit is quite different from Anna's viewpoint, Jesse's position, and Campbell's and Julia's judgment. The result is a rounded, dramatic narrative.

Flashback/Flash-Forward

Several characters use flashbacks and flash-forwards as part of their narratives. Flashbacks look back in time, while flash-forwards describe future events. The only major character in the book who does not get a voice in the main chapters is Kate. She speaks only in the prologue and epilogue, eight years after the novel's end. In the prologue, she talks about how she imagined killing her sister and that she only existed in relation to Anna. In the epilogue, Kate describes what happens after Anna's death.

Most of Sara's chapters present flashbacks. In each chapter, she primarily describes Kate's illnesses and treatments, but she also includes some information about her family. She begins with when Kate was diagnosed with cancer, then goes through each relapse, until she reaches present day and the court case. These flashbacks show Sara's increasing tension and desperation to keep Kate alive.

Campbell also incorporates flashbacks in his sections. When describing his teenage relationship with Julia, his flashbacks are set in italics. In these memories, Campbell describes how the relationship got started, what kind of people he and Julia were as teens, and important events in their romance. The flashbacks emphasize the importance of the relationship for Campbell, while underscoring how remote it is in his everyday life.

Heroes and Anti-Heroes

In *My Sister's Keeper*, Picoult contrasts the actions of heroes with those of anti-heroes. A hero is a primary character that displays commendable traits such as courage and integrity. Anna is a heroine because she takes action to give Kate what she wants. The whole point of her lawsuit is to bring her sister peace, though it costs Anna much in her life. Characters like Jesse and Campbell can be defined as anti-heroes. Anti-heroes have the reader's sympathy despite their flaws, and while not villains, see themselves as social outcasts, distrust the world, feel helpless, and lack courage and integrity. Jesse defines himself by his rebellious acts: arson, drug use, stealing cars, and supporting Anna's seemingly mutinous lawsuit. Though he does some good things, most of his time and energy is spent in self-destructive, self-serving acts.

Campbell is better adjusted than Jesse, but he bucks the system in his own way. He takes on Anna's case primarily because of the publicity it will bring him. Campbell wants to win the case, not necessarily because it is the best thing for Anna, but because it is a challenge. He also is dishonest about who he is to nearly everyone. Many people ask about the dog, but it is not until Campbell has a seizure in court that he admits to having epilepsy. Campbell also bowed out of his relationship with Julia years earlier, and he does not tell her why he ended it until she sees his seizure. Campbell keeps the world at a distance with cold and cowardly behavior.

Designer Babies and Genetic Planning

In interviews describing the origin of *My Sister's Keeper*, Picoult talks of a news story from 2000. On August 29, 2000, Adam Nash was born. He was considered the world's first "designer baby." Like Anna in the novel, Adam was conceived for a specific purpose. His six-year-old sister Molly had an uncommon type of anemia, a genetic disease called Fanconi anemia (FA), in which the body cannot make healthy bone marrow. Doctors gave the child only a year to live. Medical professionals recommended to her parents, Jack and Lisa Nash, that the best chance for Molly to survive was to receive stem cells from a genetic match. Though the couple could conceive naturally, fifteen embryos were created via in vitro fertilization (IVF) with the couple's sperm and egg in a laboratory. Two embryos were perfect matches, and one was implanted in Lisa Nash. It became Adam.

After Adam's birth, stem cells from his umbilical cord blood were transplanted into Molly. Doctors hoped the stem cells would become bone marrow inside Molly and give her a functioning immune system. Though the transplant worked and Molly recovered, the means of and reason for Adam's creation became an international controversy. There were two ethical issues involved: Should anyone be created just to provide assistance to someone else, and should embryos be screened for selected traits?

Critics saw such genetic planning as a new form of eugenics and a violation of natural law. Others believed it would lead to parents screening embryos for characteristics such as eye color and intelligence. Some medical professionals raised the question of how the family would feel about the child if his donation did not have the desired effect. Lisa Nash was certain she did the right thing, telling Josephine Marcotty of the Minneapolis *Star Tribune*, "This technology had to be brought to the forefront so people with Fanconi anemia or any other [genetic] disease know there is a way to have a healthy child."

Because of the success of Molly's transplant, some experts believed that more and more embryos would be subject to pre-transplant genetic diagnosis (PGD). PGD was developed in the early 1990s by scientists working in Great Britain and refined over the next decade. In this procedure, "cell clusters" created by in vitro fertilization are examined for genetic markers. In 2000, about twenty-five genetic diseases could be identified by PGD. Between August and October 2000 alone, at least three hundred babies conceived with IVF in the United States underwent PGD. However, there have only been a few cases worldwide similar to the Nash family's. For example, in 2002, a couple in Leeds, England, was given permission by the British government to screen an embryo to be free of the faulty gene which cause thalassaemia, a disease of the red blood cells, so that the resulting infant could be used to help an older sibling.

Not all parents are using genetic planning for the interests of other children. A 2002 article in *Washington Monthly* cites a deaf lesbian couple who only wanted a congenitally deaf sperm donor so they could have deaf children. Both of their children were born deaf. Their choice contributed to the debate over genetic planning for children. Observers worry that parents will want to control their children's appearance using such genetic testing, as well as gender, personality, interests, and sexual orientation. Genetic enhancement is also another possibility as PGD and similar techniques are refined and enhanced.

In an editorial piece in the British publication the *Spectator*, Bryan Appleyard brings up a central issue to the debate over designer babies, one touched on in *My Sister's Keeper*. He writes,

> We will … design our babies. They will certainly be no better than us and, with luck, no worse. The best we can hope for is that, having designed them, we can still find it in our hearts to love them. But that, I think, may turn out to be the real problem.

Guardian Ad Litem

In the novel, Julia acts as a Guardian Ad Litem (GAL) for Anna in her case against her parents. The Latin term means "guardian at law." GALs are appointed by the court and ensure their clients receive due process and have their feelings and opinions known in court. A GAL is usually a lawyer, but can be any adult who has received special training. The latter are usually called Court Appointed Special Advocates (CASA) or Volunteer GALs. In Rhode Island, the setting of *My Sister's Keeper*, the GAL speaks on behalf of the interests of a minor child or adult with special needs in court cases.

The use of GALs became widespread in the United State after the federal Child Abuse Prevention and Treatment Act was passed in 1974. This law requires the use of GALs in court cases involving abuse or neglect of a child. States will not receive federal funding for child abuse and neglect prevention and treatment programs unless they provide GALs for such children. It took several years for the use of GALs to be widespread in the United States, though the level of compliance from state to state is inconsistent.

Critical Overview

Like many of Picoult's novels, *My Sister's Keeper* was generally embraced by critics for its gripping exploration of emotionally complicated issues. For example, Tom Jackson of the *Tampa Tribune* represented the sentiments of many reviewers, declaring "*My Sister's Keeper* is a gut-wrenching, melancholic work designed to linger in the minds of its readers long after they have finished it." Others, such as Kim Uden Rutter of the *Library Journal*, called it "timely and compelling."

Many critics praised the way Picoult presents the story's dilemmas. Jennifer Reese of *Entertainment Weekly* commented, "*My Sister's Keeper* crackles when the characters wrestle with unanswerable moral questions." Similar sentiments were expressed on the Picoult's construction of the novel. While Andrea L. Sachs of *People Weekly* commented, "Picoult's style borders on the poetic," Robin Vidimos of the *Denver Post* noted, "It's a busy story, but Picoult keeps all the balls in the air and the story moving at a good clip. This book may be Picoult's breakout book, moving her from a book-group favorite to a wider audience."

A number of reviewers took issue with the number of narrators used. For example, Tamira Surprenant of *Capital Times* (Madison, Wisconsin) wrote:

> The device is effective to a certain

degree, and *My Sister's Keeper* is a quick and enjoyable read, but there are almost too many narrators. The story would not have missed a beat if the romantic interests of Anna's attorney had been left out.

Some critics, like Katherine Arie of the *Washington Post*, were also critical of the novel's pacing, though she felt multiple narrators were necessary to fully understand the story, noting:

The novel's shifting points of view also help to add depth to a cast of characters who would otherwise seem rather thinly drawn. Without this device, Anna's mother could become a one-sided study in shrill desperation, and Anna's lawyer, Campbell, could be mistaken for a base egomaniac.

Reviewers were divided about the effectiveness of the subplot involving Campbell and Julia. Some found the storyline out of place. Echoing such sentiments, Sara Kuhl in the *Wisconsin State Journal* noted, "The relationship is distracting." *Entertainment Weekly*'s Reese added, "Soapy discursions like this dilute the effect of Picoult's sharp central narrative." Still, several critics found Campbell to be necessary to the balance of the whole novel. For example, Jeanne Ray of the *Boston Herald* noted, "Some much-needed comic relief arrives with Campbell."

A few critics dismissed *My Sister's Keeper* outright. Meredith Blum of the *New York Times Book Review* saw the book as a "soap opera," and as "some awkward combination of a sci-fi novel and a movie on the Lifetime Channel." However, most reviewers agreed with the point of view expressed in the *Kirkus Review*: "The author vividly evokes the physical and psychic toll a desperately sick child imposes on a family." The review concluded, "There can be no easy outcomes in a talk about individual autonomy clashing with a sibling's right to life, but Picoult thwarts our expectations in unexpected ways."

What Do I Read Next?

- *The Kite Runner* (2004), written by Khaled Hosseini, is a novel that also takes a first-person perspective on life-changing childhood events. The novel is set in Afghanistan and the

United States, and features several significant plot twists.

- *The Tenth Circle* (2006), by Jodi Picoult, focuses on a family dealing a problematic teenager as well as parents who must face problems in their own lives. Trixie is suffering from emotional issues, while her father, Daniel, has not fully dealt with his own teen years as well as difficulties in his marriage to Laura.

- *Vanishing Acts* (2003), another novel by Picoult, deals with a dramatic family situation. Delia Hopkins learns that the respected father who raised her had kidnapped her from her mother when she was a young child, gave her a new identity, and told her that her mother was dead. He is jailed while Delia deals with the emotional and legal fallout from the situation, including her still-living mother.

- *The Adolescent Alone: Decision Making in Health Care in the United States* (1999), edited by Jeffrey Blustein, Carol Levine, and Nancy Dubler, is a collection of essays about the issues surrounding teens in terms of medicine and how choices should be made for their health care.

Sources

Arie, Katherine, "Spare Parts: A Genetically Made-to-Order Daughter Creates a Host of Ethical Dilemmas," in *Washington Post Book World*, April 4, 2004, p. T5.

Appleyard, Bryan, "Design Fault," in the *Spectator* (U.K.), Vol. 300, No. 9265, March 4, 2006, p. 28.

Blum, Meredith, Review of *My Sister's Keeper*, in the *New York Times Book Review*, April 18, 2004, p. 28.

Connelly, Sherryl, "Organ Donor's Tragic Dilemma," in the *New York Daily News*, www.nydailynews.com/entertainment/story/184448p 159983c.html (April 18, 2004).

Huntley, Kristine, Review of *My Sister's Keeper*, in *Booklist*, Vol. 100, No. 9-10, January 1, 2004, p. 790.

Jackson, Tom, "Latest Breeds New Life for Family," in the *Tampa Tribune*, April 25, 2004, p. 4.

Kuhl, Sara, "Author Tackles Sacred Topic," in the *Wisconsin State Journal*, May 9, 2004, p. G5.

Marcotty, Josephine, "Siblings' Transplant a Success," in the Minneapolis *Star Tribune*, October 19, 2000, p. 1A.

Picoult, Jodi, *My Sister's Keeper*, Atria Books, 2004.

Ray, Jeanne, "This One's a *Keeper*," in the *Boston Herald*, May 9, 2004, p. O42.

Reese, Jennifer, "Issue Dispenser," in *Entertainment Weekly*, April 2, 2004, p. 68.

Review of *My Sister's Keeper*, in *Kirkus Reviews*, Vol. 72, No. 2, January 15, 2004, p. 58.

Rutter, Kim Uden, Review of *My Sister's Keeper*, in *Library Journal*, Vol. 129, No. 5, p. 108.

Sachs, Andrea L., Review of *My Sister's Keeper*, in *People Weekly*, April 12, 2004, p. 63.

Seitz, Stephen, "Hanover Author's Novel Offers Ethical Dilemma," in the *Union Leader* (Manchester, New Hampshire), March 28, 2004, p. E1.

Surprenant, Tamira, "*Sister's Keeper* Thought-Provoking Girl Serves as Medical Donor for Ill Sibling," in the *Capital Times*, March 26, 2004, p. 11A.

Vidimos, Robin, "Legal Intrigue Explores Family Dynamics of Novel, Thorny Issues," in the *Denver Post*, April 4, 2004, p. F10.

Further Reading

Ball, Edward D. and Gregory A. Lelek, *100 Questions & Answers About Leukemia*, Jones and Bartlett Publishers, 2002.

> This guide, written by an expert on and survivor of the disease, offers practical information about leukemia, its treatment, and support for victims.

Eveloff, Scott E., *Both Sides of the White Coat: An Insider's Perspective*, iUniverse, 2000.

> This memoir, written by a medical professional, explores the effect of the life-threatening illness of Eveloff's son on the entire family.

Fitzgerald, Helen, *The Grieving Teen: A Guide for Teenagers and Their Friends*, Fireside, 2000.

> This book offers practical advice for teenagers to cope with people who are dying, the death itself, the funeral or wake, and their feelings in the aftermath.

Hope, Tony, *Medical Ethics: A Very Short Introduction*, Oxford University Press, 2004.

> This guide summarizes the basic issues in contemporary medical ethics, including genetics and

reproductive technologies.

CPSIA information can be obtained
at www.ICGtesting.com
Printed in the USA
BVHW041214291221
625096BV00011B/591

9 781375 384995